The Healer's Handbook:
Inspiration for INFPs

Photo by Andreas Hensel, pixabay.com

SANDRA NICHOLS

Contents

For INFPs everywhere.

The Healer

Image by John Hain, Pixabay.com

The Healers' gift is to mend the separations that break their hearts.

Separations among people and within the systems they employ are the INFPs' call to action.

The INFP motto is this: whoever needs, gets.

An INFP's empathy is an innate facility arising from an acute awareness of human suffering and an understanding of its cause.

INFPs heal by administering infusions of kindness and compassion wherever they sense the need and they do this with selfless devotion.

Healers make sacrifices that the recipients of their care are often totally unaware of.

INFPs approach a problem by imagining what an issue would be like if given more love and attention.

One of the most remarkable traits of the Healers is their ability to create wholeness by uniting diverse elements.

An INFP's most rewarding work involves improving something he or she cares deeply about.

Find your healing niche and there you will find your bliss. Be sure to search in uncommon places.

Ignore any suggestion that you are wasting your time on a lost cause. For Healers, there is no such thing.

Whatever angers an INFP most becomes what he or she learns to mend in
a unique way.

You will always feel better when you make someone else feel better.

If you give as much to yourself as you give to others, you will be able to give
even more to both.

Healing is a form of energy that can be practiced in many ways, from
watering a dry plant to comforting a friend.

The extroverts urge us by saying, if it feels good, do it. The Healers warn us
by saying, if it doesn't feel good, don't do it.

Learn to tell people you're taking a day off for yourself and follow your own
advice.

Learn to say help me and observe the response. The ones who come to your
aid are the treasures of your life.

The selfless Healers have a natural defense mechanism for combat fatigue:
sleep. Fortunately for them, sleep is one of their favorite pastimes and they
indulge in it liberally.

When it comes to self-care, the Healers must learn to practice what they preach.

There is no badge of honor for self-sacrifice if it makes you weary.

The Dreamer

Image by Stefan Keller, Pixabay.com

"If you don't imagine, nothing ever happens at all." American author, John Green

If dreaming was nothing more than whimsical fantasizing, there would be no progress.

Brainstorming sessions originated in the minds of INFPs.

"Imagination will often carry us to worlds that never were, but without it we go nowhere." American astronomer and astrophysicist, Carl Sagan

A novel idea is an INFP's greatest victory.

INFPs do not chase dreams. They create them.

The life of an INFP has more stages than the Tour de France.

Subcultures are a Healer's place of respite and adventure.

The INFPs have no difficulty being alone with their thoughts in a room full of boisterous people.

INFPs welcome change for its promise of possibilities.

There is no limit to the INFPs' ambition when their ideas raise the prospect of opportunity.

"Not all those who wander are lost." English writer, J.R.R Tolkien

Wander off the beaten track, every chance you get.

Avoid multiple choice surveys. There are never enough options for you to choose from.

Spend as much time as you want dreaming of progress. Making things better is what you do best.

Always stick to an unscheduled lifestyle.

The best dreams for INFPs evoke the thrill of expectation.

The Idealist

Image by Besi, Pixabay.com

"Life without idealism is empty indeed. We just hope or starve to death".
Pearl S. Buck

Ideals are the foundation of all great plans.

INFPs come to a decision when they consider the greatest good for the greatest number of people.

The intensity of INFP loneliness is in direct correlation to the distance between their ideals and their manifestation.

An INFP's interest is in the ideology, not the minutiae.

An ideal is not perfection. It is the best that is possible.

Healers seek the ideal but they do not have to be one.

The Healers' purpose is to improve some aspect of the human condition that has broken apart and, to them, nothing is beyond repair.

"What if" is an INFP's favorite phrase.

Never tell INFPs to think outside the box. They invented that concept.

If you are an INFP, you hold high expectations of yourself. Consider if they are worth it.

Always carry a notebook. You have far too many ideas to remember them all.

When you think about what you should be doing, you suppress the liberation of your ideas.

Unscramble something and you'll feel better for doing so.

Expect adversity. Expect suffering. Expect to learn from both.

The status quo was made to be broken.

The people who make fun of you or your ideas are not worthy of your attention to them.

Enjoy the ideal of doing nothing.

Most people want the best of what's going around. INFPs want the best that is yet to come.

If INFPs were to set the same expectations of the people in their lives as they do for themselves, they would not have many friends.

The Romantic

Image by Jo Justino, Pixabay.com

Love is the strongest force of energy. Therefore, the loving romantic cannot possibly be weak or vulnerable.

If you tell a romantic Dreamer what to do or how to do it, prepare for battle.

Conformity stifles the Romantic's spirit.

Don't choose a lover who cannot appreciate idealism unless you need a
sparring partner.

If a partner makes you feel invisible, find someone who can get over
themselves.

If someone says you're weird or your ideas are bizarre, thank them from the
bottom of your heart for recognizing how special you are.

Just because you are selfless, it does not follow that you do all the work in a
relationship.

Let go of the ones who make you feel small. Look for the ones who make
you feel at ease. Choose with the one who makes you feel valued.

At the heart of a romantic's fury is the defense of a truth they hold dear.

INFPs are romantic rebels who defend freedom, truth, and equality with
stunning intensity.

You cannot expect most people to appreciate your romantic ideals. Find the
ones who do.

Love who you were, what you have become, and what you will be.

Look for love wherever you go. If you can't find it, change location.

When someone starts a sentence with, you should, smile and respond with the three little words, no thank you, just before you walk away.

Honor your esoteric nature.

Your aim is to protest humanely.

Threaten a Romantic's right to freedom and you will witness an epic storm.

If anyone tells you how you should be feeling, ask them if you can borrow that rule book.

Decide if you wish to wait eternally for someone to reciprocate your kindness.

Even if you don't have much money, add something romantic to your surroundings. You'll feel better.

When you can't decide which one to buy, choose the most romantic one.

Choose a lover whose affection extends beyond the bedroom.

A romantic fantasy is an antidote for banality.

When the thrill is gone, so is the INFP lover.

The Truth Seeker

Image by Pexels, Pixabay.com

The Healers are drawn to the dark where the truth resides.

The insights of an INFP silence the noise of popular opinion.

The INFPs have a panoramic perspective of the forest from which they determine what's wrong with all the trees.

"Beauty is truth, truth beauty,--that is all/ Ye know on earth, and all ye need to know." John Keats. Only an INFP can figure that out.

Phonies are your rivals. You are not expected to like them nor heal them. Instead, treat the root cause of their deception.

Never waste your healing powers investigating a perpetual liar's claims unless you're training to be a fraud investigator.

Discovering the truth behind someone's persona is an irresistible temptation for an INFP.

Your best friends are genuine, humble and kind, no matter what else may bother you about them.

Avoid braggarts. You don't like them anyway.

If your job entails too much bureaucracy, you can stay, if that doesn't bother you, but that will never happen.

INFP skepticism is the impetus for their truth-seeking missions.

True crime and biography were made for INFPs.

Never ignore your instincts or first impressions. The INFP model comes with a built-in lie detector you can trust.

Find as many truths as you can. They will lead you to your purpose.

"Be yourself. Everyone else is already taken." Oscar Wilde

When you disclose your insecurities, you immobilize them.

Stay true to form and you'll always like the shape you're in.

When you think you're not good enough, try to remember who told you that lie.

If someone is ungrateful, they probably see your selflessness as a reminder of their own lack of it.

Truth is the essence of things. It is pure and unchangeable.

The extroverts want to know who it is. The artists want to show how it is. The pragmatists want to learn what it is. The Healers ask why it is

The Humanist

Image by Stefan Keller, Pixabay.com

The INFP personality is a combination of radicalism and humanism.

The condition of humans intrigues INFPs far more than their company.

INFPs are hypercritical of systems, not people. When they are criticized, they are shattered.

INFPs cherish their most meaningful human encounters and remember them with clarity.

INFP Healers believe that benevolence is the true nature of human beings and they seek to unravel the masquerades that conceal it.

INFPs are forgiving of others and they are magnets for opportunists.

The INFPs are intrigued by human beings and inspired by their progress as a species.

When human beings fall from grace, an INFP is there to catch them, figuratively and literally.

It is fulfilling for a Healer to contribute in some way to the evolution of the species.

INFPs are forgiving of everyone except themselves.

What is best for humans is what drives the Healers.

INFPs are on the outside, observing human commotion from a safe distance, studiously mapping the divisions of mankind, focusing on those who are lost, and dreaming of plans for their rescue.

Reserve most one-on-one human interactions for those you love and cherish.

The root cause of some form of inhumanity will reveal an INFP's healing objective.

Beware of those who misuse their power, but know they cannot have yours.

Do not fear those who seek to divide and conquer. Know that they represent the condition you hope to change.

Ignore those who are boastful. Egotists thrive on attention.

If you feel awkward in a room full of strangers, introduce yourself to the person with thc warmest smile.

The Optomist

Image by Pradip Kar, Pixabay

"If you can dream it, you can do it." American entrepreneur, Walt Disney

INFP optimism is an instinctively-felt awareness that things will get better.

INFPs teach us that the world is in our favor.

INFPs lead the way to a better world through their commitment to it.

Motivation among INFPs is intrinsically derived.

INFPs are optimists who worry a lot
32

Optimism is a chronic condition among INFPs.

Optimists get better with age.

Disparity gives rise to the INFP search for making the world feel better.

Every day, celebrate the expectation of something, however great or small.

History is just one damn thing after another. Move toward a better future
in your thoughts and dreams.

The world would be a far greater mess without INFPs to care about it.

The Futurist

Image by Vicki Lynn, Pixabay.com

"We are all in the gutter, but some of us are looking at the stars". Oscar Wilde

INFPs have utopian dreams of the future. Without them, they would fail to thrive.

The Healers are born futurists. They possess a world-view, an interest in progress, are multidisciplinary by nature, and have an excellent comprehension of systems thinking.

A futurist hobby or career may well be the ultimate niche for many INFPs because progress can't happen fast enough for them.

"There is some good in this world, and it's worth fighting for." J.R.R. Tolkien

See how many sources of good news you can subscribe to. Each of them contains a blueprint for a promising future.

Consume books by futurists balanced with equal doses of humanist Science Fiction.

The Flower in the Shade

Image by Manfred Richter

INFP's are the perfect paradox. They are non-conformists who want to fit in. They value authenticity, yet change constantly. They are passive creatures whose fury can ignite a small village. They deeply care about people but prefer to be alone. They are romantics who are often unhappy in love. They also wonder why they're inscrutable.

INFPs evolve continuously and help the world do the same.

INFPs want acceptance, not accolades, parity, not privilege.

The Healers create shade gardens of great beauty and possibility. The world needs more of them.

Healers are obsessed with the self, yet are utterly selfless.

Walk tall. You're more powerful than you think.

The INFPs' choice is to be in the shade where they long to be seen.

From their lonely places, the Healers learn of suffering which equips them to endow the world with their empathy.

The only places where Healers belong is where they feel they belong.

"Blessed are the meek: for they shall inherit the earth." Matthew 5:5

"Yes, I am a dreamer. For a dreamer is one who can only find his way by moonlight and his punishment is that he sees the dawn before the rest of the world". Oscar Wilde

"The future belongs to those who believe in the beauty of their dreams." Eleanor Roosevelt